of a Great Affection

Lynn,
Blessings
and Best Wishes,
Hope this strengthens
your relationship
with Christ.

Love,
Dee
+
Lawrence

Seized by the Power of a Great Affection

Meditations on the Divine Encounter

N. Gordon Cosby

Edited by Kayla McClurg

Washington, DC

Cover and book design by Martin Saunders
Cover photograph by Jean Brown
Author photograph by Sherry Castello

First Edition

inward/outward
The Church of the Saviour
1640 Columbia Road NW
Washington DC 20009

inwardoutwardeditor@gmail.com
www.inwardoutward.org

And suddenly
I was seized
by the power
of a great affection.

-Attributed to
an unknown Baptist preacher

Contents

INTRODUCTION

Gordon Cosby preached his first sermon in 1932. He was a 15-year-old high school student when he stumbled upon a rural African-American congregation in central Virginia that was currently without a regular minister. Gordon asked if he might be their preacher, and they agreed to try him out. They kept him until he graduated two years later.

Following seminary and then college, in that order, Gordon served as a World War II chaplain in the 327th Glider Infantry Regiment of the 101st Airborne Division, honing his understanding of the biblical story on the sharp-edged stone of war. In small groups, in makeshift settings—sometimes in foxholes—Gordon faced the soul-stretching questions of his age. Did the God Story of scripture have meaning in the face of human despair? Could the divine-human encounter be trusted? Did the suffering Jesus offer fundamental hope?

In 1946, back home from the war and dissatisfied with his role as minister in an institutional church setting, Gordon sensed he was not meant to follow the traditional path. He knew that what he and his wife, Mary Campbell Cosby, had dreamed of doing since their childhood in Lynchburg, Virginia, needed to happen now. They would shape a new kind of church that took seriously the gospel call to reconciliation. Their church would be an ecumenical church, embodying the full range of diversity found in Christ's body. It would not shy away from the immensity of the world's pain, nor from the immensity of the Living Word that speaks hope to pain.

Over the course of the next 62 years, Gordon read and prayed the scriptures daily and preached nearly every week, calling people into the depths of the divine encounter, inspiring them to become catalysts for creative action. About 45 missions in the Washington, DC, metro area exist today because of his teaching.

In 2008, at the age of 91, Gordon retired from the weekly pulpit, but he continued to teach and counsel and preach. He devoted himself more intentionally to building relationships with persons who had suffered, especially those returning from incarceration, finding in them a deep reservoir of wisdom and love.

Gordon wondered aloud in recent years if

excerpts from his sermons, originally intended for a congregational setting, might also have value in written form, and he asked me to discern that possibility. He was excited about this initial offering of meditations, and I regret that he will not be able to receive the first copy. On March 20, 2013, at the age of 95, Gordon Cosby passed from the earthly realm he loved so much into the utter fullness of God's Realm.

Gordon sometimes preached about what it means to be "seized by the power of a great affection," a phrase from an earlier era to describe the conversion experience. We tend to drift toward complacency and numbness. Opening ourselves to the affection of divine power heals us and restores us to life. The Great Affection leads us home.

Here you will find no explicit guide for the journey, only a few crumbs marking the trail, a few love notes scattered along the way. They are offered for our pondering, praying, perhaps disagreeing. May they remind us who we are, and whose we are. May they sustain us on the road ahead and keep us hungering for home.

Kayla McClurg

Truly Ourselves

Becoming Whole

It is a pity for life to be predominantly struggle and survival when it is designed to be love, joy, peace, excitement, wonder and triumph. All of us long to move toward that for which we are designed, but one of our serious problems is a lack of integrity.

By integrity I mean a correspondence between the truth of the faith to which we declare allegiance and the deeper living out of that truth in our lives, in the daily routines of our lives. The inner division of not living what we say we believe wracks us unmercifully.

With one genius part of us we believe the loftiest things. With other dimensions we almost totally disbelieve. These selves war within us. One thing is clear: the anxiety will remain with us until we determine which self is the deepest self around which all the other "many selves" ultimately become integrated.

Are there ways to effect this integration and thus become people of greater integrity? Can we become whole rather than fragmented? In biblical language, can we be saved? Jesus came for the express purpose of seeking and saving all that was broken, fragmented, lost. But the history of the human race is one of rebellion against the sovereign Creator God and inability to live the life for which we were intended.

Getting It Together

What are the implications of my "getting it together" within? Suppose, by God's grace, I drop my defiance and trust God to bring together my head, my commitment, and my heart—what then?

If God desires integration for me and all things, and if God has the power to get us where we need to go, then I can trust that every experience I need to enrich my life and to move me along toward integration will be given to me. No obstacle will be able to deter me.

With my focus now on the God who has the power to complete and perfect all that has been started, my anxiety lessens. I don't have to use energy wondering if we'll make it, but I can feel hope and excitement instead.

God is God, and I am Not

If God is sovereign, I don't carry the ultimate responsibility. My task is to be a companion of God, yoked with Jesus himself. Jesus has the ultimate responsibility to pull things off, so I just enjoy his presence. I spend my time watching him, marveling in a state of wonder, free, relaxed, spontaneous.

I don't have to take myself too seriously—no need for strutting, for projecting some image of myself that I hope will impress others—because God already is holding it all with utter seriousness. I can point to God when people are impressed. I don't have to carry the weight of self-image any more.

When I experience God as sovereign and trustworthy, then to live creatively within my limits makes good sense. To defy God is to defy my limits and to try to correct what has seemed to be God's great error—that I was meant to be a creator, not a creation.

But if I learn to trust, I will see that my limits are an expression of love and give me all the freedom I could ever want. I will start thanking God for the limitations of my particular circumstances, seeing them as the very set of "givens" that are right for me.

If this is who God is, then none of us will be denied anything that is really needed for our completion.

Needing God

That which was central for Jesus is so very difficult for us:

Union.
Communion.
Oneness with God.

Jesus described the poor soil of our hearts—the hardness, the shallowness, the crowdedness of our lives that make it difficult for God to penetrate to our depths, to touch our real selves. But one day, somehow, through God's patient gardening, the soil does become sufficiently prepared and something from Beyond does penetrate and take root. We are touched in our depths.

When the depths are struck, we are overcome by a hunger amounting to an inner desperation. That touch, that connection, with our true inner being—the true Beyond reality—creates an inner desperation for the Real.

We have tried so many things and we have tried so many ways, but nothing else has reached our depths and satisfied the awful inner longing. We need God—God's very Self—to touch us directly. We need to be penetrated and invaded by the Divine Reality.

Reaching out to God

The movement from the false self to God is painful. God is reaching out to us long before we reach out in return. We resist reaching out to God even when we know it is what we need and want.

When I was in my teens, I would hit one of those places that I suppose most of us hit when I would say: "All right, I've been playing around with this life long enough. I'm going to get on with it now. Now is the time to really start praying instead of just talking about it."

Then, sure enough, once in awhile I actually would start. I would take 30 minutes to pray, and oh, it was wonderful! Wonderful! My guilt would flow away because I was doing at last what I knew I should do. Every once in awhile I would even have a sense of the presence of God.

And then, almost invariably after I had had this wonderful time of prayer, sometimes within the next five minutes, everything in heaven and hell would break loose, and I would be uglier in my attitude than I could remember having been during the whole previous year! So I want to give you this warning: Don't judge reaching out to God by your own sense of it. Just keep reaching.

LEARNING TO LOVE DIVERSITY

If I can learn to love the diversity of the people God has brought to me, then I can be open to and respond to the totality of the human family. The person with whom I am having the greatest difficulty is likely the greatest gift right now in my life.

Too often we look for people, and a community, who will be most apt to meet our every need. We were denied so many things earlier in life, and now we're coming into our own and looking for the people who will support us and encourage us and never disappoint us. We idealize and even "pedestalize" a community that claims to be Christ's Body, expecting them to give us all we have imagined we need and want.

The reality is, every genuine community consists of people at all levels of capacity. The majority are deeply broken. Many there are among us, often at the edges of the community, who have been deeply hurt. They are wistful people hanging around in the hope that the gospel and Jesus might be real—almost daring the community to prove what they are reluctant to really believe.

Will they find love here? Will we be able to embody Christ in ways that will allow him to give them what they need?

Who Are We?

Who are we in our deepest origins?

At bottom we are love because Love resides in our depths. We are made, in our depths, in the image and likeness of God, who is love and light. In God there is no darkness at all. Made in that image, we are beauty, we are truth, we are goodness. What God is, we are. We are unique, we are priceless.

When we look at Jesus, we see human nature as it is intended to be. Fully human, fully divine, Jesus shows us what human nature is, what the Divine nature is.

Our goal is to go down, down and down into our own inner beauty and love, to rest in our own depths. We commit, together in community, to being more and more ourselves, our real selves.

And we commit to being more freely available to others, in long-term, permanent, unconditional belonging.

Immersed in God's Nature

In Christ, I am one who seeks reconciliation with every person. I am a peacemaker. My nature is not to extract vengeance—not even "equal" retaliation, an eye for an eye or a tooth for a tooth.

In Christ, I cannot kill, either personally or through the state. In Christ, I learn to love my enemies—personal, national and global. I prefer to suffer abuse rather than engage in contempt. I will not belittle any person, sneering at or calling him or her a fool.

I cannot support any plan to build nuclear weapons designed to incinerate millions of God's children and mar forever the beauty of God's creation. This I cannot do. To do otherwise would be to question who I am and to deny that I am in Christ.

Who am I? Beneath all other answers, I am in Christ. I am immersed in God's nature. Christ's nature has permeated and inserted itself into my deepest being. That is my core identity.

SURPRISED BY EVIL

We keep being surprised by evil. As we grow in our capacity for compassionate connection with oppressed persons, the cruelty, violence and capriciousness of pain become clearer.

We begin to feel ourselves as one with the refugees, one with the poverty of millions of the world's people. We become painfully aware that the problems are even worse than we dreamed.

We had thought if we could share the stories of oppressed persons with others, many would respond. But often they do not. We might be listened to, we might even be admired, yet others do not seem to care as much as we had hoped. Don't they see the evil in these conditions?

To know the evil hidden, and not so hidden, in the human condition makes us cautious. Cautious of the world at large, cautious of one another. Can we relax and rest and rejoice in a God who allows evil and also allows people not to care, or do we stay always on edge, uneasy, unable to trust?

We must remember: Evil happens. So does love. We choose which place we will live. I want to live in love forever.

OUR TRUE HOME

For all of us, there will come a time when our knowing and doing will be greatly diminished: perhaps memory loss will leave us with little capacity to expand our knowledge or even to recognize our loved ones, and for all of us, unless we die suddenly, we will become helpless, unable to act on our own or another's behalf. Are we no longer persons at this point? Is there anything beneath the knowing and doing?

Is there a real eternal self that we can claim now and begin to deepen and expand into forever? The determining question is whether or not this unique, deeper person exists. Is it real, although unawakened? Is there another culture that is uniquely suited for each of us and that calls forth our inner truth, who we really are?

We can keep living from the shallow, surface self or we can claim the real, the deep, the inner self where the Spirit of God already dwells. Only then do we become free. Only then will we experience the freedom that Meister Eckhart says comes from "needing to *know* nothing, *will* nothing and *have* nothing." This inner place of freedom is our true home.

Belonging to Each Other

We Are Connected

There is no such thing as an individual. Many of us operate under that assumption, but separateness is a mental concept which holds no reality. We are persons connected—not just to *some* people and things, but to *everything*. This is, by our very nature, simply who we are.

I am not saying that it would be lovely if we *could be* connected; I am saying, we *are* connected. Whether or not I like the idea, I belong to you. Whether or not you like the idea, you belong to me. We belong to all creatures, and all creatures belong to us.

It takes practice to see this way, and I suggest we start with those we find most repulsive. Several people have asked me if they might begin instead with those they find less repulsive, but my response is always "no."

Unless we start with the most repulsive people we know, we will never reach the totality. We have to get comfortable with the thought that we really belong, in depth, to the total creation. This is why, scripture tells us, Jesus lowered himself to be with us. He wanted to belong to all of who we are. Even in our most repulsive condition, he wanted to be covenanted to us.

He who was rich, for our sakes became poor. He did not reluctantly accept our poverty, our filth, our brokenness. He embraced and welcomed us. "Blessed are the poor," he said. We are blessed when we can recognize and accept our own poverty and one another's.

As we consciously let God within us flow and as we interconnect with God in others, we experience ourselves as bonded, not only to each other but in the divine relationship. We experience the "is-ness" of the whole, thus extending the flow of eternal life—the eternal realm—into this realm. We prepare our souls for the climax of belonging.

This is not a sentimental idea, but the way we are made. We belong to each other. We are joined.

Now I Am a People

Jesus of Nazareth, in his incarnation, was homeless. He had a community of women and men who provided for him out of their means so that although he had no home, he had a community—a continuity—of caring.

In his present homelessness today, incarnated in thousands of weary persons barely alive on the streets of our cities, he does not have that continuity of caring. On the streets today, those with whom Jesus wanders and struggles for survival often are mentally ill and unable to sustain intimate relationship.

Jesus' present homelessness is much worse than his earlier homelessness in Palestine...unless we will be his community. Can you see in your imagination Jesus and all of his broken friends? Can you see how they would respond to the safety and love of community?

When we live into the vision of safety and love for all, then *all* of us will experience inward healing. All of us will be able to say together, "Once I was nobody, but now I am someone. Once I was a part of no people, but now I am one of God's people."

GOD'S DREAM

There is no ideal community. There never will be.

We all have the capacity for projecting what Dietrich Bonhoeffer called our "wish dreams" onto a hoped for community. We arrive with our exit strategy already prepared. As soon as we start to see the community in all its immaturity and brokenness, we will have decided already on some good reasons to leave.

Even now, after more than 50 years of trying to be faithfully a part of community, I can't believe that such a tiny handful of people can create so many problems and hurt so many. A person has to wonder, is it worth it?

But God, in Jesus, has not given up. God's dream is for a church, a faithful community which will guide a desperate humanity into God's future for us all.

I want to be a part of that broken people marching into God's future. For without a people, in spite of my own new birth, I inevitably will be sucked back into non-being. Without the community, I will die.

WHAT IT MEANS TO BELONG

To belong to a church is to set oneself down more deeply into the person and being of Jesus Christ, and into a particular segment of people.

To belong means to give inner consent to being inter-penetrated by other people in order to become a cell in Christ's Body, a cell which gives to all the other cells, a cell which receives from all the other cells.

To belong means the old sense of individuality slips away. The "I" becomes "we." What used to be the individual "I" flows into this people, and they flow into me. What used to feel like distinct boundaries are no longer clear. There is a merging of life.

In spite of my discomfort, I am eager now to be known. I trust others to hear and accept the full depths of me. I am willing to reveal myself. Despite the hurts of this revealing, I will not withdraw.

Then one day I see it: I have surrendered my rigid need for autonomy. I belong to a larger whole. No longer are things marked as 'mine' or 'yours.' There is nothing to defend, nothing to protect. To belong is to enter a new space of freedom.

"YES" TO CHRIST AND TO CHRIST'S PEOPLE

> I commit my life and destiny to Christ, promising to give him a practical priority in all the affairs of life.
> *- from the original membership commitment of The Church of the Saviour*

There is an inwardness and depth and intensity and totality in our commitment to Christ that makes it a forever experience. We are grasped by the eternal and ultimate, and to be so grasped is to belong forever. To commit to this One who is both with us and beyond us is to give myself away in love forever. The only question is how to surrender myself even more totally to this passionate love.

We are called permanently to Christ—today, tomorrow and even after death—a continuing journey of giving and receiving, giving and receiving, love. We who belong to Jesus Christ know that we belong to him through belonging to others who also are called to be his Body in the world today.

To say 'yes' to Christ is to say 'yes' to people. To know Christ as God is to be organically, integrally part of a community, and to be ultimately responsible to Christ is to be responsible to others in Christ's Body. Together we show the world who

Christ is, until the entire broken human race will respond to the love of God manifested in that Body.

Christ continually pours himself into us, not just to each of us individually but to all of us corporately. Thus, to break away from one another is to do violence to him and to the family he has brought us into.

Something mystical happens when we commune. Something eternally serious happens when, in his name, we are received and we receive another into the family. This is no human club or society. No, we literally become members of one another—organically bound forever. We will place no limits on the ways we learn to give ourselves to one another.

Unlimited Liability

Numerous claims come upon me. The particulars of each claim on my time and energy and attention are guided by many considerations—other competing claims, my finitude and limited capacity, my understanding of the moment. What I want is to give to each all that I can give with no arbitrary limits. Especially I want as few limits as possible with each of you.

I want to give you unlimited forgiveness, unlimited prayers, unlimited money, unlimited emotional and spiritual support—in general, I want to give you unlimited liability. In Christ, I want to never leave you nor forsake you.

It's easier for us to demand that others assume unlimited liability for *us* than it is for us to offer unlimited liability to *them*. We see how gluttonous we are, how unending our own needs are, and we know how burned out and exhausted we will be if, in addition to everything else we are responsible for, we also take on the needs of others.

But unlimited liability means to be willing to care for the other in ways we will not demand for ourselves. It is to know that Life is grace. Life responds generously to gratitude and our willingness to pass along the grace that comes to us. Life never responds to demands.

The particulars might change, but the unlimited liability of our love for one another will only ripen and deepen through the years, and throughout eternity. The bonds between us can never be broken. The changes between us have no power to destroy us.

I will not lose you. You will not lose me. We will be there for each other—in the ultimate "there" where God dwells—forever.

DIVINE ONENESS

The Christian community is not to be just an accepting community. It is to go past the point of simply accepting a person where he is and to a point where it knows oneness within its life, just as Christ knew oneness with God—God perfectly in him, and he perfectly in God.

Oneness was Jesus' thing. The world will never believe that anything divine has broken into our life until they are aware of this divine oneness in us.

The oneness Jesus was pointing us to is not uniformity; it is not submissiveness. Conformity is not oneness. Oneness happens when each person is living from his or her own uniqueness and individuality.

A person who gives herself utterly to God in Christ, and gives herself utterly to the Christian fellowship as a place to grow, is freed so that her own distinctiveness can at last come to birth. This person is not caught up in the temptations to conformity, but together with others is on the path to divine oneness.

The Intimacy of Forgiveness

At the Heart of It All

If we are in Christ's family, we are in intimate relationship with one another. We have been promised to each other, to be close to one another in this new family forever.

These are the people who now have the power to really hurt us.

We are all so new at loving. We are all so immature—such beginners in the business of love. We stumble around, hurting one another in unintentional but creative ways. The only way a community can hold closely together is through forgiveness.

For Jesus, forgiveness was at the heart of everything. In his own little group, the beginnings of the church, not a single person understood fully what he was about, even after three years of his loving and teaching them. One even betrayed him. One denied ever having known him. None stood by him at the end.

And what did he do? How did he respond?

He forgave.

A Common Destiny

It is difficult to sustain and deepen long-term relationship even when we choose the partner. How much more difficult it is to sustain deepening relationship with those whom God brings together to be a local expression of the Body of Christ.

Especially when we are brought together from every strata of life—educated and uneducated, "cultured" and "uncultured," of varied races and ethnicities and cultures, of opposing political persuasions and theological understandings, rich and poor. It is difficult, if not impossible, to sustain a life together.

The poor see the rich insisting on their beautiful homes and various luxuries, and the rich see the poor striving for what they themselves already know will not satisfy. The rich are inwardly torn by having access to a style of life that once felt natural but now seems questionable in light of the poor's deprivation. The poor are inwardly torn by coming to know a different kind of deprivation experienced by the rich.

To really belong to one another and to depend on one another—to really share a common destiny—is difficult for a community that wants to be diverse. It is also the community's only hope of survival. Whether or not we will be honest with each other, whether or not we will let ourselves be truly known, determines everything.

HIGH HOPES ...

People—especially those close to us—have the power to deplete us. Our closest kin and friends have the greatest opportunity to hurt us. We are all clumsy lovers. In our clumsiness we hurt each other; we get hurt by each other.

We know people are not meant to be alike, yet we want those we love to see life as we see it. To have the same base of values, to see from the same perspective, as we do.

The intimacy of our family life, our work relationships, our faith community, is such that we sometimes feel pressure not only to know and be known by others but also to accept the uniqueness of each one's very being, despite how well that uniqueness fits with our uniqueness.

Others are given the power to drain our joy unless we can allow all persons, all groups, to be who they are—including their clumsiest and most hurtful behaviors that offend us. We might need to choose a different kind of connection with people whose heinous and outrageous behavior offends us, but we must choose to forgive them for that behavior if we want to live in the joy that is our birthright.

… AND GREAT DEMANDS

We love people. And because we care, we long for all people to become what they can become. We place hopes and expectations on the ones we love. Then a strange thing happens. Hopes and expectations shift and become demands.

We demand that our hopes and expectations be realized, and we cannot forgive people (or causes or institutions) for not being what we know they are capable of being. We are disappointed. Our spirits sag.

Not only do our hopes and expectations for others change into demands, but we also become demanders of ourselves.

I say to myself, "I've had such great hopes for you, Gordon. You have so much potential. You should be at a place of greater inner maturity by now. You should become what I know you're capable of becoming. How can you still be working with what you're working with at your age?"

I have not yet met my hopes and expectations for my own life. I have turned my longings into demands and thus I have taken the risk of being terribly disappointed.

It is difficult to be joyful if I am always disappointed in others and in myself. I must forgive others for not being what I know they could be, and I must forgive myself for being where I am at this stage of my life. I must never let hopes and expectations turn to demands.

God's creatures are not meant to make demands or to be demanded of. By nature we are receivers. God gives, and we receive. We practice receiving with gratitude, with joy, with open hands. Placing demands on others, or on ourselves, drains us of the possibility of experiencing life as grace, as gift, as abundance.

Ready for the Impossible

After Jesus forgave those who had been unable to stand by him, he commissioned them to carry forgiveness into the world. In forgiving them, he was preparing them for ministry, which is always to take on the impossible.

A genuine call for any individual or group is always going to be "impossible" because a genuine call is never something we are prepared to take on. It is never something that depends upon our strength and stability. Instead, it stretches us beyond our imaginations.

God wants to give us a vision beyond any vision we've ever known. Together with the broken victims of this city, God wants us to dream new possibilities and share those dreams with political and civic leaders. God wants everyone to have a part.

God wants the addicts to be healed and the prisoners to be freed, the poorest children to be taught in the finest educational system and the sick to be treated by the finest of medical care, and all of them together to become catalysts for new structures that will benefit everyone.

Who is going to give servant leadership to our city? Who is going to be the salt and the light for our society? The church, of course. You and I, and all God's awkward, gifted, ill-suited people. With all our limitations and liabilities. We are the ones who have been given the great commission to continue Jesus' calling. Of course it is humanly impossible. That is a given. Whenever God calls, the call, in our understanding, is impossible.

But God will be the one at work, not us. God is the healer, not us.

Dwelling in Gratitude

As we face our own need, as we go inward and repent of our own brokenness, as we sense the awfulness of our own bent toward living independently and not in intimacy with God and others, then we are able to withdraw our projections we have put on others. We can begin to dwell in gratitude for those pilgrims who, even in their own struggles, even in their capacity to offend, have been given to us for this period of our life's journey.

The person I have experienced as a particular challenge then becomes exactly the one I need right now. Suddenly I am able to consider the possibility of what a wonderful person this is! What a gift to be part of this remarkable community!

I begin to see the very people who annoyed me as privilege, as gift. I realize that I literally am being sustained by them. I can bear in community what I could not bear gracefully without community. Now I have the capacity to see the uniqueness of each person as more important than the brokenness.

It takes no special grace to see the weaknesses, the foibles, the wounds of other people, but it takes a special grace to see the indescribable beauty, the courage, the inner spirit of another, especially someone whose wounds and weaknesses seemed central before.

God has done and is doing an amazing work with many of us. It is important that we see it, marvel at it, rejoice over it, and enjoy the beauty of each person, thanking each one for being the companion pilgrim God has given us right now, for this unique passage of our journey.

Instead of demanding perfection, we will now see the inner beauty that already resides in each one, and the gift that each one has been given simply to bless us on our way. Even if the blessing is given harshly, we can begin to see beyond the words, beyond the actions.

We will see the inner core of one another and be able to express our true gratitude. The flow of love will increase between us, and from us to others, and we will be changed in deeply significant ways.

A Few Human Problems

Most of us struggle with a few human problems for most of our lives. They keep popping up again and again. Perhaps they are never put finally to rest. They are our individual problems and yet also universal.

Growing, evolving human beings must always be concerned about these personal/universal issues. Each of us could make our own list, but I find six recurring human problems which, for me, don't go away:

(1) *Loneliness* – the inability to bond with other people, feeling cut off and without deep connection. Even though our lives are jammed with good relationships, mysteriously enough there remains a deep ache and longing, a homesickness, within us.

(2) *Sin and guilt* – sometimes vague, sometimes clear, but always a sense of what my life might have been had I remained constantly close to the essentials of life rather than becoming too often diverted from seeking first the kingdom of God and God's righteousness. What might have been possible had I earlier in life been radically responsive to Jesus' command to follow him? I have a gnawing sense of how much others have suffered because my life has only partially flourished.

(3) *Keeping an appropriate balance* – work, play, rest, worship, service, study, relationships. All of these create urgent demands. Sometimes we give up and say an unbalanced life is unavoidable; it is just the way things are. We say we will endure as gracefully as we can. But we can't help but wonder what it might mean if we could find greater peace within and among all the strands of what we do.

(4) *Maintaining a spiritual temperature* – hot enough to be contagious with excitement and hope, yet cool enough not to burn people unnecessarily. Do we excite others with the fire of the gospel? Are we a welcoming presence or do we turn people away?

(5) *Guidance* – knowing what choice to make in any given moment. The choice I make can change the direction of my life and the people with whom I am connected in community. The moment comes; the moment goes. The decision I make, or don't make, reverberates endlessly.

(6) *Death* – the inevitable moment that all other moments are leading us toward. What awaits us? What is the appropriate preparation? Am I preparing for this immense journey of journeys?

These are some of the ultimate issues of my life, my personal yet universal concerns that keep me seeking forgiveness.

Forgive us Our Freedom

Sometimes we say that a community of acceptance means we can be ugly to each other any time we want "because we are like family." We say, it is so wonderful here to be free, to be able to be myself; others will have to accept me and love me just the way I am.

Well, it is mighty wise to choose carefully who you are ugly to! Maybe you will be ugly to someone who has a strong sense of self and enough love of you to be able to absorb your ugliness, but more often the ugliness gets poured out on someone who is not able to add your neediness on top of his own.

The act that is for you a sign of freedom can be the very thing that diminishes another. Just a little thing, maybe, but worth noticing as we try to learn how to love and forgive.

These things are going to take a lifetime. They won't be done in a year or two. Some of us are going to have to decide, in our pursuit of freedom, to put our roots down deeper. Whatever it costs us, for the rest of our days, we will have to let God stretch our capacity. Whatever is required of us, we'll do.

The Great Love

ONLY LOVE

In the struggle to become Christ's Body, we have one weapon and one alone: Love.

Any other weapon betrays the cause.

We are not allowed demanding, controlling power. We are not given the power to fix things. No violence, no hatred. Just love.

We have to love. We have to love those who pervert our message and even kill us. We have to love God's possibility alive in each one, even within the enemy. We have to love the Beyond beauty captured uniquely in each person.

Only love. Love, love, love, scandalous love. Love like that of a Lamb slain from the foundations of the world.

Love is what first softened your heart and mine. Love brought us into the struggle. Love alone has the power to break hearts open so that we will all lay down our defenses and join in the cosmic movement toward a new heaven, a new earth, in a Holy City whose foundation is Love.

Our Deepest Essence

The deepest essence of each of us is love. At bottom, we are made in God's image, so if God is love, then I am love. You are love. All creation is love.

If I believe this, I will trust the inner revelations of love. I will treat people, all people, with love. Sensing God in their depths, I will see the numinous in them and will reverence them.

Ultimately we either reverence everything or we reverence nothing.

By nature, we co-inhere with others because God is in us. If my love and God's love cannot touch the depths in the other, then I choose to take and absorb whatever may be directed toward me of the evil in the other. That is far better than isolating myself, cutting myself off from God in people.

Isolation is sure death. The hurt I sustain from others becomes gift because it drives me more deeply into God, who is love.

Surrender

To surrender is to come to a point of conscious brokenness and pain and to cry out for help. To surrender is to accept the help that is given. Not to choose the help we think we want, nor to try to change the help that comes.

There are possibilities for newness within me which haven't yet been activated. I welcome the Great Love that life wants to send me.

I surrender to the ultimate creative power flowing into me and through me, however it is given, wherever it takes me. I no longer require a certain measure of safety or wisdom or power or possessions.

I surrender myself in total vulnerability to this moment, in ultimate trust. Whatever is given, whatever comes.

Become It

Jesus makes it crystal clear. Our work is to become love, and from the state of being love, we are to love. He sums it up this way: "Love one another as I have loved you." To fail to become love is to fail life. It is to fail to become human.

No matter how varied and rich our experiences, how honored we've been, how great our achievements, we will have missed what life was all about if we do not become love. We will not at all be ready for the only milieu that matters, the one we will enter when we are poured out at death.

I think one of the great failures of ministers like myself is that we have exhorted people to love, and we have deplored the lack of love in the world, yet we have not become love. We have not known how to instruct our own souls in the art of loving.

Suppose I really hear Jesus say: Gordon, do you love me? How will I stop answering in generalities? What will be my specific practices that will bring inner change? Has love become my primary work, my central activity, my core being?

I think Jesus is saying, if you aspire to love one another as I have loved you, then *see* one another as I have *seen* you. I see you as sacred. You are precious beyond any measure of preciousness. Accept that I see you this way. See every person you meet as I see you. Learn to experience yourself and others with reverence.

There is more in each of us that is beyond what we can grasp. Will I dare to see it? In the person who is telling me off? In the one who is trying to get closer than is comfortable, in those who are pressuring me? Will I dare to enjoy the presence of the sacred even in those who annoy me?

To love is not to try to solve anything about a person, not to try to fix a person. It is not to *do* so much as to *be.* Just be open to God's sacred creation. Just love what is.

INTENSIFIED LOVE

God longs to enter and give us the gift and pleasure of intensified love. But there is a fundamental condition: completely voluntary inner consent. No voluntary inner consent—no entry.

No coercion, no pressure, not even overwhelming evidence can force God's entry. God has infinite respect for the dignity and individuated self of each human person. God knocks. God waits. God longs to enter but never forces entry. God is patient and will wait forever.

Even when we have been loved faithfully, we have trouble believing that anyone could love us to such an extreme and stand by us under duress. We are conditioned to expect non-love, to anticipate limited love. Yet God refuses not to love. All God knows how to do is to take the risk of love.

If we are saved by grace (which is God wanting to penetrate our deepest being) through faith (which is inwardly letting ourselves down into that love when we're not sure of it), then we can relax into God's affirmation of love. We simply rest in God; we are filled with God.

God, and only God, becomes our compulsion, our obsession. God is all in all. Any separation from this love is death.

Letting God Love Us

God initiates love, and we simply respond in love. When we love God, it is only because we are reflecting God's love already given. We are able to take the active step of loving God, and God in one another, only as we are able to let God love us. Then, and only then, can God produce in us that kind of life which makes us for the first time wholly alive as responsible human beings.

Until we love this way, we are not truly human. We are not fully alive until we know the freedom which comes from love.

Letting God love us, rather than trying harder, always harder, to love God, frees us for the highest form of activity, which is to love. Letting God love me, allows me to love you. Allowing God to love us turns us toward serving sacrificially, forgiving, sharing and sympathizing, lifting up the fallen and restoring the bonds of community.

I don't know why it takes us so long to get hold of this. The Gospel very plainly says we will never love more by trying harder to love more. We will love because we have basked in God's gift of love, because we have relaxed into the sheer joy of letting God love us.

Love Power

Most communities have few experienced lovers. Few of us have ever been loved unconditionally, so we are much more at home using other kinds of power—non-relational power, unilateral power that can be controlled from one direction. This kind of power seeks its own advancement and protection. It seeks to control outcomes, produce results, fix ourselves and fix each other.

Love power is different.

Love power is when you let your own inner being flow out toward others, and you welcome the flow of others' inner beings into you. Love power is letting yourself be shaped and changed by the other. Love power is being open, vulnerable, defenseless, letting the new emerge, never knowing ahead of time what God's next thing will be.

The love power of genuine relationship changes us. God flows into our deepest being, and we flow into God's. There are no clearly defined boundaries. We are changed by the flow, and by the new thing God is doing.

Love is being willing to be changed by the other without needing to control what those changes will be. Love is trusting that our inner being will be enlarged and enhanced by taking into ourselves the inner being of another.

To be a giant of a person is not to do mighty and impressive acts, but to allow others into our hearts and imaginations and to be expanded and enlarged by them. In love, I can take you into me and not lose myself but be infinitely enriched.

When we flow into one another in this way, we never know where we will be taken together. That's the excitement of our enterprise. The most impressive witness of the early Christians, when people from outside their fellowship looked at them, was the depth and the quality of their love.

This will always be our central witness. For God is love, and to be in God is to be love.

Come Home

Across the eons, God calls out to us:

I love you.
I want to be with you.
I want you to be with me.
I will never rest until
we fully belong to one another.
You are my beloved.

I have loved you from before
the founding of the world.
I am lonely until you rest fully in me.
I am calling you to come home.

Haven't we all, in some way or another, left home? Can any of us say that our hearts are constantly at rest and at home?

Who can say every moment is peace, love, exuberant joy because we are at home with the One who loves us? Who can say we are inwardly at rest in God and look forward only to new realizations of that love?

Very few, because we have left home. And now, again, still, we are being called to return to the Great Love from which we began. To make the journey home, to return from the far country to which we have wandered, is to stop searching for unconditional love where it can never be found.

It is to stop condemning ourselves and others for what we cannot give. It is to surrender at the feet of Infinite Mercy.

Enfolded in the embracing arms of this love, we know we are where we are meant to be. Totally at ease in the present moment, not wanting anything, we reach our destination.

Here we are safe. Here we are home.

Just the Way We Are

This community can never be perfect. That will come later, when the interim period—which we call life—is over and the hope of glory has been consummated. So don't expect things to be perfect now.

But isn't it amazing that, even now, someone chooses to love us as we are? Isn't it remarkable that anyone could love us, could want to be reconciled with us and us with each other? Why in the world would anyone want to love me just the way I am? Or love you just the way you are?

The only thing I can figure out is that the Holy Spirit must really be here, among us. Somehow, through no special power of our own, we are letting the Spirit of Christ teach us how to love even when we feel unlovable. And this enables us to enter continually into the immeasurable depths of God's love and to share that experience with each other.

Suffering and Compassion

LIVING UNDER PRESSURE

This is an era of living under pressure. Everybody is trying to know everything and trying to do everything. We are trying to be in touch with what is happening all over the world. We are trying to care on a grand scale. We also have the instruments, and the capacity, to make each other's lives miserable on a cosmic scale.

We are in turmoil. The anxiety level throughout the world is near panic, and sometimes it moves beyond panic. People operate blindly out of their panic. In our deeps we know the world is playing Russian roulette, and the next chamber fired might end life as we know it. Though we try to numb the fear, no drug is adequate.

In addition, many of us have taken on the pain of the oppressed—those oppressed by poverty or abuse, the mentally ill, the elderly, the homeless. For those who let themselves be sensitized and who begin to struggle valiantly against "Pharaoh"—the dominant consciousness—the pressure increases.

The toll for many of us is extremely high, and some of us find we cannot pay it. Some of us have difficulty sleeping, or we have psychosomatic symptoms of various kinds. We are tired and heavy much of the time, near burnout, but determined to be faithful to the end. And so there is "oughtness" and duty in our trying to hold on.

Is there relief from the pressure that threatens to do us in? Can we learn to "be with" yet also "detached from" the events and people that threaten to overwhelm us? Is it possible to detach from, and yet also attach to, the world's pain?

Is there any balm in Gilead? Is inner peace in the midst of suffering really possible?

KNOWING ANOTHER'S PAIN

Compassion is to know the pain and suffering of others. Not to know *about* the suffering and pain of others, but in some way to actually know that pain—to enter it, hear it, taste it, let it in.

We talk about getting in touch with our feelings, and that is central to our freedom. The complementary step is to get in touch with the feelings of others. This necessitates getting into their frame of reference, their way of perceiving.

Others' way of seeing might seem wrong or distorted, yet it still is their experience of life. To see the way others see, to enter their inner world and feel with them, requires the development of an imaginative capacity.

In part, knowing that someone understands and feels our pain *is* the relief we need, even if nothing more can be done. To know that someone feels with us the pain that we feel is to have the nature of that pain changed and made more bearable.

Compassion for another's pain will always begin individually and personally. But we also must learn to institutionalize our compassion. We should expect systems to support our desire to be compassionate.

We must move beyond personal caring to the kind of caring that creates corporate structures to combat apathy and self-seeking. Expressing compassion individually and personally is necessary, and so is creating compassionate structures for all.

We can do it. There are innovative and imaginative ways that we, as spiritual entrepreneurs using technology and creative means, can stem the increasing suffering of the world. We have not yet applied all our resources to the benefit of the poor. We have not yet seen it as a fundamental command.

God is in pain. We must learn to celebrate life by celebrating the God who is in love with all of life and, through this pilgrim band of followers, longs to ease the world's pain.

Deep Realism

Jesus said you cannot love and serve the dominant consciousness—the order of darkness, disorder and violence—and also belong to the realm of light and order and love. Simply put, you won't be able to dominate and control others if you are giving yourself away, to the point of laying down life itself.

But no matter how genuine our surrender, much of the dominant consciousness lingers in us. As we grow in our capacity for compassion and are able to connect with oppressed people, feeling with them their poverty and despair, we also become more aware of the cruelty and violence of our world.

We wonder: Is God really as loving as we thought? Does God really have ultimate power?

Jesus knew a deeper reality. He had an intimate acquaintance with evil; he knew that the wheat and the tares grow together, that evil exists wherever there are expressions of the good. Jesus cautions against protecting ourselves from the evil around us.

Face the possibility of the worst; it really can happen. Discovering evil in the midst of compassion is to be expected. It doesn't invalidate God's love for you.

So Much Need

Every true disciple of Jesus is going to be surrounded by devastating need. Sometimes it is a need for bread; sometimes it is a need for clothing; sometimes it is a need for emotional support. What amazes me is that some of us seem so surprised by the needs. The surprise surprises me.

Time and time again, I have heard people say, "I have never seen so much need in one place as in this church." But isn't this the hallmark of the Church, that it will always be surrounded by people in need? If it is not surrounded by agonizing, heartbreaking need, then we have been unfaithful to the One who is the Lord of the Church.

One of the greatest tributes ever paid to Jesus was intended as a smear. He was called a friend of publicans and sinners—a friend. Before we try to feed the crowds surrounding us, we must first ask if any of them are my friends. Do we love them? Do our hearts ache when we see the crowds, or do we mostly feel impatient?

All that's required is to bring the little bit we have—not the radiant, mature personality we do not yet possess, not the human capacity to fill every need. He simply asks us to offer what we have right now, to start where we are.

All Creation Longs to be Freed

Perhaps our deepest alienation from God is our alienation from the creation. Strange, how completely most of us have been cut off from the creation, and how much violence we have perpetrated against her, this amazing created order that God has given us.

Scripture says that creation has been suffering, just as people have been suffering, because of our oppression. Do we really hear this? It is not only people but *all creation* that has been groaning and suffering.

The created universe longs to be freed, longs to be healed.

The destruction of the natural environment corresponds to our illnesses, what we call the diseases of civilization.

Each of us, in our own bodies, carries the pain of the ecological crisis.

Jesus' Passion for the Poor

We create Jesus in our own image and around our own perceived needs, but there is no Jesus other than the Jesus who lived his life from a position of passion for the poor.

Passion for the poor was not just one of many things about which he was concerned; it was central to his deepest being.

We say that Jesus incarnates in our historical time/space realm the very nature and being of God. Not just that he was an especially compassionate man who liked to be with the poor and sided with the poor, but that he incarnated God. And God's very nature is always to opt for the poor.

In prayer, we seek to be open. We open the door of our heart for God, Jesus and the Holy Spirit to flow in and sup, dine, dwell with us. We offer an empty inner space so that God may flow into our very being.

So, the vital question is this: What kind of God are we inviting in?

We can only invite one God—the God of compassion who is on the side of the poor and the victims of the structures of the world. This is the nature of "I Am." There is no other.

THE GREAT COMPASSION

The compassion we perceive in Jesus might be as if we heard Jesus say:

God embraces your inwardness.
Your inner being is a part of God's inner being.
We carry you in our heart.
We feel with you, we suffer with you.

Your loneliness, your emptiness,
your sense of failure,
your brokenness and despair,
your inner damage and hurt,
your visions and longings,
the indebtedness to life you carry
and haven't been able to pay back,
your anger because your life hasn't
become what you had hoped—
all of your inner being is carried in our being.

It is all here. In us, healing is possible.
In us, you can rest. You are safe.
Trust me.

Love Knows How to Stoop

Isn't it strange how, even among the people of God, we clutch people rather than love them?

Love knows how to take a basin and a towel, how to stoop and meet the needs of the disciples, how to meet the needs of the world. A person will never be at home in the Christian church until he or she learns to how to be at home with a basin and a towel.

I am talking about having a sort of flexibility, so that when needs arise we can see the need in our imagination and leap to the need as a fish leaps to the bait, eager to be of service.

Until this is what we are doing with all of our days, and all of our nights, we will not fully belong to one another, because to belong means to know how to take a basin and a towel, and to serve.

The Really Real

Remember the Deeps

We pay a high price for consciousness, but the price is even higher for unconsciousness.

There is a surface level of reality and a deeper level, the level of perfect peace, wonder and surprise. This deeper level can be touched now, not only at some later opportune moment. The surface swirls with events, circumstances, problems, worries. Its tasks seem impossible and overwhelming.

In the deeps, something else is taking place.

In the deeps, the resurrection body is forming. In the deeps, there is no confusion, no complexity. There is only the present moment and the one thing we are, in this moment, to see and revel in and do.

The surface of life is always with us, and the deeps are always with us, too. By planting the stakes of our lives down into those deeps, we can begin to experience a restful detachment from the swirling events on the surface.

It's a matter of learning to withdraw our energy from the multiple crises on the surface of our lives and focusing our energy in the deeps. In this way we come to be rooted in transcendence, not needing to know anything, not needing to do anything, not needing to possess anything.

In the deeps, we require no minimal comfort level, no minimal level of support from others. We simply enter the infinite realm of grace. Every surface distraction is forgotten in the process of remembering the deeps.

THE REAL WORLD

Through no choice of our own, we were born into the existing culture of a particular period of history, and we have taken on the traits of this culture. We have lived by its rules and understandings; it has seeped into our inwardness. It all seems very natural and real. Most of us have had no one to tell us that this world is not real at all. It is the *unreal* world.

Often, as we conclude a retreat at Dayspring, someone will say: "This has been powerful. I hope I can hold onto it back in the real world." But the "real world" is not the one to which we are going. We return to the "unreal" world where the culture is distorted and trapped in pretense. The "real" world is the one we were just in, where our hearts were opened and we gave inner consent to rest in God.

To return to our routines in the dominant culture is to go back to the *unreal* world, not the Real one.

The time is coming when the unreal world will not even be remembered. All that will remain is what is Real. Make no mistake. What we usually call the real world is not Real at all. It is as flaky as they come.

Laugh at it; weep over it; pray for it; take every opportunity to expose it; seek to redeem it. But never make the fatal mistake of thinking it is *Real*.

What if We Truly Believed?

Consider the lilies of the field.
Relax into God's infinite bounty.
You will be taken care of.
You are safe.

God is very friendly.
The manna will be given.

What would it mean for us if we believed promises like these? What if we could deepen our sense of being intimately connected to the unseen world beyond this world, the "really Real" world?

When we do make that connection, when we know that we will be sustained, taken care of, nurtured every moment, we are in the eternal flow of Life. We will live with a sense of awe and amazement and wonder and delight.

So tune in to the Real. And be carried.

THE GRACE OF BEING

To be, at all, is an unspeakable privilege. The bottom line of reality is the grace of being, and knowing fundamentally that God and life are *for* us.

> Nothing can separate us from the love of God in Christ Jesus our Lord.
> *- Romans 8:39*

Life is grace heaped upon grace. It is inconceivably good, and at its conclusion we will wonder why we ever wasted any time in heaviness and complaining. To live the truth of life is to celebrate and rejoice.

To live the truth is to play. It is one of the ways we celebrate God's amazing goodness.

Jesus spent a lot of time playing. Those who, in their compulsive moral goodness, were unable to understand the importance of play called him a wino and a glutton. But he was just enjoying the goodness of life. He knew where all of life had come from and where it was going.

In fact, just 30 years earlier he had come from that other Realm, and soon he would be returning to it. Even the misery around him, even his own impending torture and death, were unable to depress him. The irrepressible spirit of the compassionate Jesus knew how to celebrate each moment.

In his name and by his Spirit, I hereby commission all of us, especially those of us who live under the weight of heavy burdens:

Play!
Life is good!
Nothing can separate us
from God's love!
All is grace!

Disillusionment and Hope

Life is a series of disillusionments. To be disillusioned is to have our usual ways of seeing the world stripped away. The world turns out *not* to be the way we wanted it to be or how we felt it ought to be. As our hope in Christ grows, we are given new degrees of disillusionment.

The more clearly I see what kind of world is possible, if only we loved one another and allocated our resources for human need, the more disappointed I am in my country, in our churches, in my own community, for not doing so.

The more I care about the particular lives of particular people, the more I am disappointed by the gap between our desire to live reconciliation and our general inability to love. It is quite a feat to continue to allow myself to be disillusioned and yet, at the same time, to be filled with a burning hope.

Follow and Pray

Keep following. Keep your feet on his way. Remember, he said: "I am the Way." Not, at the end of the way you will find me, but I AM the way. As soon as you get started on my way, you will find me. I am the way right beneath your feet, wherever you are, at whatever point you start. If you start from the gutter, there I am with you. If you start from the peaks of worldly success, there I am with you.

Keep following, and then, keep praying. Often people will say they don't pray because God doesn't seem "real" to them—I guess they feel like they're just talking to themselves. But I say that perhaps God does not seem real *because* they do not pray. Who would try to communicate with us if we show no interest in listening?

Especially when it feels unreal, especially when you don't want to, pray. Prayer opens the door between the seen and the unseen. The very reality of God, for me, depends upon waiting, listening for God's voice. If I fall away from this attitude of listening, then the secular fog descends upon me and the very idea of God becomes unreal.

Keep following, keep praying, keep loving. If we can live in this spirit even a little, we are touching the ultimate principles.

The Obsession

Lord, out of the depths
I have called to you;
hear my cry, O Lord.
-Psalm 130

My deeps must be heard. Are you listening, God?

If you are not listening and longing for my deeps as I am longing for yours, it is all over for me. Lord God, I am desperate for you. I must find you. Please hear me—all of me. I can't live unless the depths of me are heard by you. I wait for that love unfailing, which I now know I will not find anywhere else.

The depths become the central obsession of our lives, the one danger we pursue, the one longing to which we give our hearts and lives. Everything else grows out of this one thing. We are given a pure heart, a single focus—God and God alone. There is no other deliverance.

Who We Really Are

A friend handed me the welcome book we have, and I looked at the comments made by several visitors recently. One was terse. It simply said, "Terrible!" Just a few lines down was another comment, and I am sure it was about my own preaching, for it said, "Very foggy."

In various ways we will be reminded who we really are, at least in the eyes of others. We are a very imperfect bunch, regardless of what expectations are placed on us. How insensitive we are to the real concerns of God and one another. The needs of people cry out in our presence, and we simply pass by.

Christ and the Church in all its glory are available to us, but we are more aware of our own awkwardness and stumbling. We carry a pain in our hearts because it is taking us so long to become like him.

Yet we also sense there could be real treasure contained in these earthenware vessels. There might be real insight and faithfulness and inspiration, at least enough to take the next steps together. Which is what ultimately mattters—that we grasp as much as we can grasp, and keep taking the next steps.

The Ultimate Unity

The beauty and wonder that I see all around me are hints of the future. My imagination is too undeveloped to understand now the glory of Shalom—the full reconciliation of God—but I know that nothing and no one will be left out of that ultimate unity.

God will wander around the universe forever until every lost sheep and every lost coin are found. No abused child, no suicidal teenager, no addicted man or woman, no mentally ill person, no political prisoner, no homeless stranger, no one awaiting execution—no one will be forgotten.

With inner illumination I feel the pain of the various segments of my global family, including the broken bodies I have to step over on Columbia Road and don't know what to do to help.

But rather than being depressed, I find myself saying, "My little brother, you're inwardly broken and outwardly your body is broken and addicted. Nobody thinks you have a future, and you don't think so either, but you're going to make it. And all of the repressed beauty of your original image, the image of God, is going to be totally freed. And one day I'll see you again, and we'll have new bodies."

This beauty of the Beyond.

NOT AFRAID

When I reflect deeply on my life and what I really want, it is not to be afraid. When I am afraid, I am miserable. I play it safe. I restrict myself. I hide the talent of me in the ground. I am not deeply alive—the depths of me are not being expressed.

When I am afraid, a tiny part of me holds captive most of me which rebels against the tyranny of the minority. When I am afraid, I am a house divided against itself.

More than anything else I want to be delivered from fear, for fear is alien to my own best interest. I want to give myself generously, magnanimously, freely—out of love. I want to be able to take risks—to express myself, to welcome and embrace the future. I want to see what it is to be more deeply me.

I want union with all of life and existence. I want to know and sense a oneness with others—with all humankind. I want to know warmth and closeness, to give acceptance and understanding and support. I want to sacrifice myself freely, for this is when I am most alive, most me. I sense that the art of loving, the art of risk taking, is my thing.

BREAKTHROUGH

You'd Better Do It

Way down deep—and not so deep for many—we are angry. We spend a lot of energy and time trying to keep our anger within reasonable limits, but once in awhile we blow, often out of all proportion to the circumstances that supposedly caused the eruption. Oh, the poor souls who are around us when the explosion happens!

Many are the reasons for anger, but one of the least understood and most important is this: the denial of creativity. Believe me, if we deny or block our creativity, we will be *mad.*

So, if you need to write a poem, you'd better struggle to write it, even if you have to eat simply and live in a garret. If you need to write a book, you'd better get busy writing it.

If you need to build a beautiful friendship, you'd better do it, even if you have to let go of a lot of other important activities. If you need to be with your child, to love her and let her know how important she is to you and to God, even if it keeps you from getting your next promotion, you'd better do it.

If you need to dig in a garden and plant a seed and watch a flower begin to grow, you'd better get to it.

If you need to build institutions which will create new neighborhoods where people may flourish, let nothing stop you.

If you need to sing a song, sing. If you need to dance, dance. Give yourself to whatever is your unique creativity, and if others do not understand, that is their problem, not yours.

You must do what you have been created to do. Why? Because God, the Creator, is continually breaking forth, flowing with limitless energy and life.

You don't have to hoard your creative resources and dribble them out little by little. You can be lavish—absolutely prodigal—in letting your creativity flow. You cannot exhaust the Creator's resources.

God is Infinite Flow

God—the being of God, the presence of God, the numinous, the holy, the ineffable—is with us and is in us every moment. God is the very medium of our existence, just as water is the medium in which the fish lives and swims.

There is not a single moment when we are not sustained and held in existence by that Presence. We forget God, but if God were able to forget any one of us, we simply would not exist.

God thinks of us every moment, cherishes us and delights in us in every moment. No matter where we are, what we are thinking or doing, that Presence beams, longing to break through.

The mystical consciousness is the instrument through which we receive into our deepest being the love that surrounds us and is seeking to penetrate us. This love energy, this presence, this hope is inexhaustible. There is no scarcity in God.

Imprisoned by Safety, Crippled for Life

Fear is the supreme crippler. It blocks our lives from flowering into fullness and maturity. It keeps us from taking the next step into freedom. Opportunity after opportunity is missed. We become imprisoned by what appears safe.

The new, the unknown, the opportunity that might or might not work out—they scare us. We hang back, remaining in the prison of the known. In time, we become accustomed to fear, tightly bound and restricted. We are crippled for life.

This happens not only to individuals but to entire neighborhoods and societies. When a society is invaded by drugs and violence, or defiance and darkness, a corporate pathology sets in. Such a society becomes predatory, and people feed on one another.

The strong prey on the weak. Children are exploited and denied creative public role models. Old people spend endless lonely hours fearful of leaving their rooms. The few who long for a new spirit and want to confront the enormity of it all often become discouraged and ultimately passive.

What good does it do to confront fear? Isn't it wiser just to co-exist with it? And so the sickness deepens until all coherence, unity and health disappear, leaving an even more pervasive fear.

People become more private, with ever more extensive security systems and isolation tactics. The police become more cautious. The business community withdraws. Community organizations no longer try to implement new possibilities. Fear becomes a debilitating, depressing and tragic condition.

Fear also can grip a nation. Its confidence and vigor are sapped. A fearful nation begins to project its fear onto others. Its creativity diminishes. The normal course is for nations and civilizations to peak and then to fall, often into total oblivion. Creativity, love, compassion are totally incompatible with fear.

Preparing for The Ultimate Journey

The really big issue of our lives is the meaning of death. What are we moving toward? Every decision, every moment we live, every experience is leading us to the moment when we will die.

To die is to usher in, to welcome, everything that has ever happened to us. What awaits us at that moment and beyond that moment? What is the appropriate preparation? What shall we take with us? Without some light on the problem, we live this life totally in darkness.

Whether or not life has meaning depends, in large part, on whether or not we can discover the meaning of death.

Who or what can help us? We don't even take off for London or Tokyo or Brussels without at least reading a guidebook about the place and the people and the history. But the immense journey into death is demanded of all of us (at a time totally unspecified) and many of us don't even ask if a guidebook is available.

When our loved ones go, we grieve and then begin to pick up our lives as if this realm is actually what continues forever. The obvious reality is that each of us will make this journey. Some of us will be making it "soon and very soon." What will help us to prepare?

As soon as I ask the question, I'm wary of the answers. I think we normally live best by sharpening our profound questions rather than coming to superficial answers. "I don't know" is perhaps the truest answer to the really profound questions. Ultimately we must live in and by mystery.

But in a profound sense, there *is* an answer. And the answer for us is the same as for Jesus, the one we call Lord. Jesus became fully human. What we are up against in our lives, he was up against. He, for our sakes, became one of us. By what code did he live? How did he work with life's biggest questions?

He lived in deep, personal, relational intimacy with the Divine, the one he called *Abba.* He talked to Abba. He listened to Abba. He obeyed Abba. He wanted only to do Abba's will and to be true to the divine nature he was embodying.

Abba was self-emptying, so he was self-emptying. Abba was loving, so he was loving. Even when the price to pay was death by torture, he continued to love. He refused to betray the nature of Abba.

This is how we prepare for all the passages of our lives...and for the ultimate passage.

God Breaks Through

It is in prayer that God breaks through to us and connects and reveals God's self. It is in the personal presence of God that we sense ultimate Presence and are given the vision of what God is up to.

Call is being drawn into, gathered up into, active participation in what God is up to and is going to complete. Since call is central to all that we are and do in this community, let me remind us of several things which are at the very heart of the nature of this meeting with the biblical God in the person of Jesus.

When Jesus comes to us, God comes, the Holy Spirit comes. We meet the triune God. Since our tendency is to create and worship idols, it is important to be aware that we are receiving the revelation of the authentic God.

The central revelation is that the triune God is a God of justice—justice for the whole earth. Justice is a fundamental dimension of love.

God always hears the cries of the oppressed, the victims of injustice. God hears the cry of the poor. When the real God breaks through to us, one of the signs will be our deepening passion for those who are mistreated by and the victims of the powerful.

This God is in the midst of the suffering. So how can we not be there, too? God longs for us to share our resources sacrificially; to be active advocates for the children, the jobless, the homeless, the elderly; to raise money; to advocate for legislation which will make this a just nation.

When we are given the vision of God's justice for our nation, we will give our lives to further that vision. If you are not intimately involved with someone who is oppressed under the power systems of our nation, don't let the week pass without getting to know such a person. That friendship could be what saves your life.

Dying into the Real God

Am I ready for the new thing God is doing?

Ultimately this question is the question at the end of all questions: Am I ready to die, to transition into the vast realm of glory?

In light of this ultimate question, what is the meaning of my life today? What shall I give attention to right now?

My readiness for the ultimate moment of transition depends upon how I respond today. It is crucial that I give myself to God, which means to attend to my true self as opposed to shoring up my false self. And that I give myself unreservedly in love to others.

Too often, rather than working with these big questions, we make ourselves some idols. We worship small, impotent gods who can't ultimately deliver us. We create false gods, gods who will protect our greed, who even say our greed is justified.

These gods won't be there for us when we die, yet we keep ourselves busy fashioning them after our own image and around our own perceived needs.

The real God, the delivering God, cannot be fashioned. The real God fashions *us.* The real God speaks a real Word, an imperative Word, and that Word still speaks today.

The real Word of God says:

Be with me.
I will not abandon or forsake you.
Leave your privilege.
Leave the systems that reward you
for not being faithful to my way.
Create a new system—
be in true covenant with me.
Lose your life to really live.

PART OF EVERYTHING

Our task is to drop our hostility and our estrangement from the creation and to begin to rest in it. To connect with it. To give it our friendship. Our work is to nurture creation, and to be nurtured by it. To meet God through it.

Every mist that settles upon the earth, we draw from. We connect to it. Every time the sky is beautiful or imposing, every time it rains, every tree that we see, every flower that we notice—if we connect, there will be no moment that we are not being renewed. It's not only a matter of spending 60 minutes at the beginning of the day listening for God. Everywhere we go we pick up messages from God. We are renewed. We stand in awe.

Because we are connected—connected to God, connected to each other, connected to nature—we are part of everything and everything is part of us. We respect all things and love all things and reverence all things.

If we can live this way, consciously and intentionally, then death is just about the easiest passage imaginable. We simply move from this friendly dimension to the next friendly dimension. From love to Love. It is a beautiful experience. We can relax. We are safe.

May It Be So

Sometimes we make religion much too complicated. Christianity, at bottom, is the simplest religion that ever existed: "Love is of God, and everyone who loves is born of God and knows God."

Keep following, keep praying, keep loving.

If we do these three things, and persist in doing them, day after day, week after week, whether we feel like it or not, then one day we shall find suddenly that the mist of history and personal doubt will have vanished.

We will become aware of the presence, radiant and strong and real. The radiance will flood into our lives, the One Among Ten Thousand, the Bright and Morning Star. May it be so.

About the Author

GORDON COSBY was the founding minister of The Church of the Saviour in Washington, DC. Noted for more than 65 years of prophetic preaching and teaching calling people of faith to a fuller embodiment of God's vision for the world, Gordon lived a simple yet profound life dedicated to following Jesus in the active pursuit of God's realm "on earth as it is in heaven."

From his youth Gordon was called to a more radical expression of the gospel than traditional church structures allowed. Home from serving as a chaplain in World War II, where he had seen how unprepared young men were for life's greatest challenges, he dedicated himself to the dream of a different kind of church. In 1946, together with his wife, Mary Campbell Cosby, and seven others, that dream began to take root, leading to the first membership commitment of The Church of the Saviour in 1947.

Gordon's preaching challenged the Church to live more deeply rooted in the "real Jesus" who did not shy away from the social and political arenas and who showed special care for all who were oppressed. He noted that the spiritual life is composed of two journeys, inward and outward, interwoven in community.

Gordon was both a dreamer and a doer, starting small churches, organizing non-profit ministries, seeking the common good—always from a posture of large leisure. At the time of his death he was a member of the Church of Christ, Right Now, whose mission is to dismantle the prison system and be in community with returning residents.

About the Publisher

INWARD/OUTWARD offers writings about the spiritual journey in community—inward, into the depths of the true self, and outward, into the depths of the world. A project of The Church of the Saviour, inward/outward provides:

- excerpts to educate and inspire;
- reflections on scripture;
- writings from The Church of the Saviour community.

To subscribe or to learn more, visit us:

www.inwardoutward.org
www.facebook.com/inwardoutward.